A Kid's Guide to Drawing America™

How to Draw
District of
Columbia's
Sights and Symbols

Aileen Weintraub

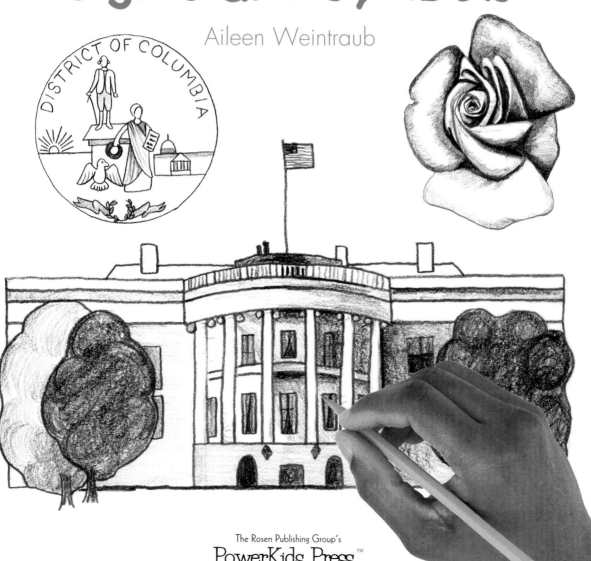

The Rosen Publishing Group's
PowerKids Press™
New York

Published in 2002 by The Rosen Publishing Group, Inc.
29 East 21st Street, New York, NY 10010

First Edition

Editor: Jennifer Way
Book Design: Kim Sonsky
Layout Design: Mike Donnellan

Illustration Credits: Emily Muschinske
Photo Credits: p. 7 © Adam Woolfitt/CORBIS; pp. 8–9 © collection of the Washington County Museum of Fine Arts, Hagerstown, Marlyand, gift of Joseph Brewer; pp. 12, 14 © One Mile Up, Incorporated; p. 16 © Associated Press/AMERICAN PRESS/Shawn Martin, member; p.18 © Eric and David Hosking/CORBIS; p. 20 © Joe McDonald/CORBIS; p. 22 © Joseph Sohm; Visions of America/CORBIS; p. 24 © Bettman/CORBIS; pp. 26, 28 © James P. Blair/CORBIS.

Weintraub, Aileen, 1973–
        How to draw District of Columbia's sights and symbols / Aileen Weintraub.
                p. cm. — (A kid's guide to drawing America)
        Includes index.
        Summary: This book explains how to draw some of District of Columbia's sights and symbols, including the district seal, the official flower, and the Frederick Douglass National Historic Site.
        ISBN 0-8239-6063-3
        1. Emblems, State—Washington (D.C.)—Juvenile literature   2. Washington (D.C.)—In art—Juvenile literature   3. Drawing—Technique—Juvenile literature   [1. Emblems, State—Washington (D.C.)   2. Washington (D.C.)   3. Drawing Technique]   I. Title   II. Series
        743'.8'99753—dc21

Manufactured in the United States of America

CONTENTS

1	Let's Draw District of Columbia	4
2	The Nation's Capital	6
3	Artist in District of Columbia	8
4	Map of District of Columbia	10
5	The District Seal	12
6	The District Flag	14
7	The American Beauty Rose	16
8	The Scarlet Oak	18
9	The Wood Thrush	20
10	The White House	22
11	Japanese Stone Lanterns	24
12	The Frederick Douglass National Historic Site	26
13	The Capitol	28
	District of Columbia Facts	30
	Glossary	31
	Index	32
	Web Sites	32

Let's Draw District of Columbia

The District of Columbia, also known as Washington, D.C., is the capital of the United States. It is a city that is not part of any state. The U.S. Constitution gives Congress the power to govern the district, because District of Columbia is also the home of the U.S. federal government. Residents elect their local officials, however.

Because District of Columbia is not a state, Congressional representatives for the district do not vote in Congress, as do representatives from the states. The district has a mayor and a city council. Some parts of the district, such as utility companies, are run by the federal government.

Engineer Pierre Charles L'Enfant designed Washington, D.C. Benjamin Banneker, an African American scientist and mathematician, helped to perfect L'Enfant's design. The district was designed to be the nation's capital. The streets are centered around the governmental buildings.

After many of these buildings had been constructed, a war broke out between Great Britain and the United States. This was known as the War of 1812 (1812–1815). British troops burned many of the buildings in District of Columbia, including the White House. These buildings had to be reconstructed.

In this book you will learn to draw the sights and symbols of District of Columbia. Each drawing starts with a simple step. Every additional step is shown in red. To shade an area, tilt your pencil slightly and rub back and forth. Let's get started.

You will need the following supplies to draw District of Columbia's sights and symbols:

- A sketch pad
- An eraser
- A number 2 pencil
- A pencil sharpener

These are some of the shapes and drawing terms you need to know to draw District of Columbia's sights and symbols:

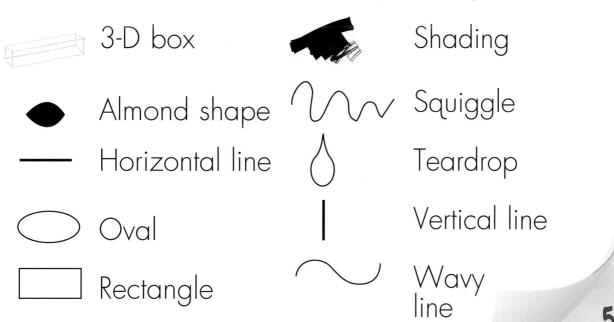

3-D box

Shading

Almond shape

Squiggle

Horizontal line

Teardrop

Oval

Vertical line

Rectangle

Wavy line

The Nation's Capital

District of Columbia represents democracy to the American people. It is the place where lawmakers from around the country come together to make decisions about the nation's laws. The district's motto is *Justitia Omnibus*, which is Latin for "justice to all." Many of the 606,900 people living in District of Columbia work for the U.S. government. Tourism is a major industry for the district. People from all around the world visit District of Columbia each year. Visitors to District of Columbia can take tours of the White House, the Capitol, and the Supreme Court Building.

District of Columbia is also known for its museums, its monuments, and its historical sites. Among the many monuments is the Washington Monument. It is modeled after an Egyptian obelisk, a tall decorated column with a pyramid-shaped top. The Lincoln Memorial and the Jefferson Memorial are two other monuments that pay tribute to important U.S. presidents.

Visitors to District of Columbia can take tours of many governmental buildings, such as the U.S. Supreme Court Building. This Greek-style building was designed by the famous architect Cass Gilbert and was completed in 1935.

Artist in District of Columbia

Henry Livingston Hillyer

Henry Livingston Hillyer was born in 1840 in Utica, Ohio. As a child, he loved to paint. He made his brushes out of hen's feathers and his paint from powdered brick dust, chalk, and washing blue. When Henry was ten years old, his family moved to New Jersey. A few years later, his father sent him to New York to study with an artist named A. D. Shattuck. By the time Hillyer got married in 1865, he had painted 137 canvases. He painted scenes from nature. His sketchbook shows pictures of plants, trees, and streams. In 1866, he traveled through Europe to study art. Throughout his life he had trouble selling

Hillyer sketched *On the Potomac* in one of his notebooks. He often did pencil sketches to prepare for making a painting.

his paintings. Many times he painted new paintings over ones that he had not sold. Hillyer did this because he could not afford to buy new canvases.

In 1873, he moved to District of Columbia. There he organized the Washington Art Club. He also began working in his own art studio where he painted many scenes of the Washington, D.C., area. Hillyer died of malaria in 1886. Today his paintings are exhibited at the Washington County Museum of Fine Arts in Hagerstown, Maryland.

Hillyer's *Near Washington, D.C.* captures the soft light of the landscape. This oil-on-canvas painting from about 1880 measures 7" x 11 ½" (18 cm x 29 cm).

Map of District of Columbia

Map of the Continental United States

District of Columbia's area is only 68 square miles (176 sq km). It sits on the Potomac River in the eastern part of the United States. Maryland borders the district on the northwest, northeast, and southeast. Virginia is across the Potomac River to the southwest. The weather is mild in District of Columbia. Winters average about 37°F (3°C). Summer temperatures can be very warm. The district is divided into four quadrants, or parts, the northwest, the southwest, the northeast, and the southeast. These quadrants meet at the U.S. Capitol. Parks are a major part of District of Columbia's landscape. There are 753 parks within the district!

1

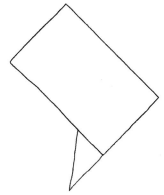

To draw a map of District of Columbia, begin with a tilted rectangle. Add a triangle to the bottom left corner of the rectangle.

2

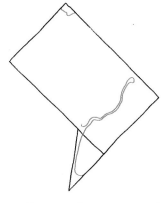

Add the small curved section in the top corner of the rectangle. Draw the curvy line for the Potomac River.

3

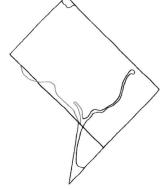

Add more curving lines along the western part of the district.

4

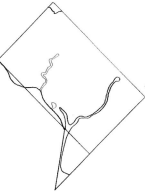

Add one more section of the river and the small, round shape for the river's basin.

5

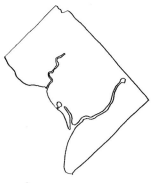

Erase extra lines.

O	U.S. Capitol
	Frederick Douglass National Historic Site
	Potomac River
△	Potomac Park
▭	White House

6

Add some of District of Columbia's sights:
a. Draw a circle for the Capitol.
b. Draw a house shape for the Frederick Douglass National Historic Site.
c. Shade the Potomac River.
d. Draw a triangle for Potomac Park.
e. Draw a rectangle for the White House.

The District Seal

District of Columbia has a local government, but Congress has the power to veto, or to reject, new laws that the local government may want to make. Congress may veto a proposed law when local legislation could have a negative effect on how the district operates as the nation's capital.

Because the district is the United States's capital, it was slower to develop its own symbols, such as a flag or a seal, than were many of the states. The legislative assembly of the district made the seal official on August 3, 1871. The seal includes a representation of the Capitol, the American eagle, and the figure of Justice placing a wreath on a statue of George Washington, the first president of the United States (1789–1797).

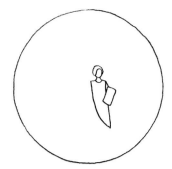

To draw the district's seal, begin with a big circle. Draw the outline of Justice's hair, head, neck, arm, tablet, and dress.

Complete the dress. Add Justice's other arm holding a wreath.

Add the basic outline of the Capitol. This can be done using a half circle, a short line, a few rectangles, and a triangle.

Next draw the eagle using curved triangles for the wings. The body, the head, and the beak can be made using ovals. The tail feathers are made with upside-down U's. Add the Sun on the left side of the background.

Add the words "DISTRICT OF COLUMBIA" along the top of the circle. Then start drawing the statue of George Washington standing on his platform. Notice how the statue is behind both Justice and the eagle.

Finish George Washington by carefully making curved lines. Add a wreath and a banner at the bottom of the seal.

Add the shield by drawing a U with a rectangle on top and vertical lines inside the shield. Shade your drawing, and you're done.

The District Flag

After District of Columbia became the nation's capital, many unofficial flags were used to represent the district. In 1920, it was decided that one design should be chosen for the official flag. The final design was chosen on October 15, 1938. A. E. Dubois headed the commission to find a design for the flag. This simple design was taken from a shield that appeared on the coat of arms used by George Washington's family. A coat of arms is an arrangement, usually on a shield, of several symbols that represent a family. The district flag has two red horizontal stripes and three red stars on a white background.

1

Begin drawing the flag with a rectangle.

2

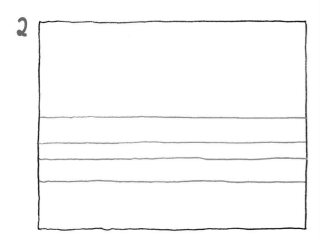

Add four horizontal lines. These will be the flag's stripes.

3

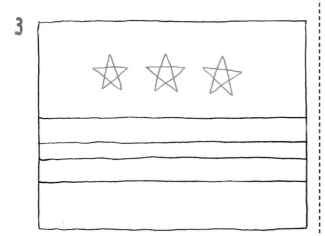

Add three five-pointed stars in the center of the area above the stripes.

4

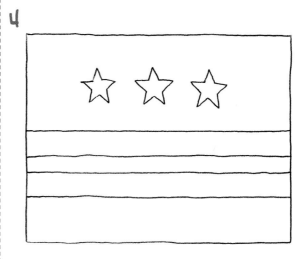

Erase the extra lines inside the stars.

5

Shade the stars and the stripes. Great work!

15

The American Beauty Rose

The American Beauty rose is District of Columbia's official flower. Roses have long, thick stems and green leaves. The rose is often referred to as the Queen of Flowers. Depending on its color, a rose can symbolize many things, such as love, friendship, beauty, and peace. American Beauty roses are dark pink in color. The dark pink of the American Beauty rose represents gratitude and appreciation. Roses grow best in sunlight, and they need a lot of water.

1

Start drawing the American Beauty rose by making the center of the rose. Draw a small, almond-shaped spiral.

2

Add another soft shape that curls around the first spiral.

3

Add two more soft, curling shapes.

4

Add another spiral of petals. Notice that the petals begin to get larger the farther they are from the center of the flower.

5

Add two more soft, bending shapes on the right side of the rose.

6

Draw the large petal on the rose using a wide, heartlike shape.

7

Now add the other three large outer petals.

8

Look carefully at the photograph of the rose to see where the darkest and lightest areas are. Shade your rose. Beautiful!

17

The Scarlet Oak

The scarlet oak (*Quercus coccinea*) became District of Columbia's official tree on November 8, 1960. It is named the scarlet oak because the leaves of this tree turn dark red, or scarlet, in the fall. The tree's leaves grow to be from 3 to 5 inches (8–13 cm) wide. The fruit from this tree is the acorn. It takes two seasons for the scarlet oak's acorns to ripen. Many animals, including birds and squirrels, eat acorns. When the bark of the scarlet oak is young, it is a smooth, light brown color. As the tree gets older, the bark's color darkens. The inside of the bark is often red. The scarlet oak can be found in many of the parks and along the streets of District of Columbia.

1

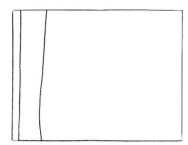

Let's draw a close-up of the leaves of the scarlet oak. Make two horizontal lines for the main branch of the tree.

2

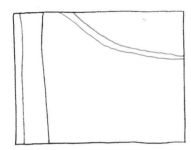

Add another, smaller branch hanging down.

3

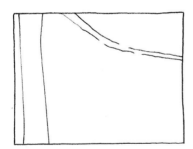

Erase three areas of the branch, and follow the drawing carefully. This will make space to add the smaller branches.

4

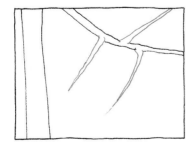

Add three more branches.

5

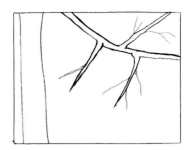

Add thin, wiggly lines for the thinnest branches.

6

Next add a lot of leaves. Notice where the leaves come to points. Draw the veins running through the center of each section.

7

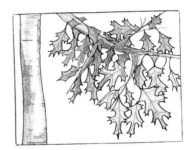

Shade the tree. Notice that some of the leaves are darker than others. Great work!

The Wood Thrush

The wood thrush (*Hylocichla mustelina*) is the official bird of District of Columbia. These birds are about 8 inches (20 cm) long. They are brown and red and have small eyes. They eat fruit, insects, snails, and even small salamanders! These birds often sit on low tree branches, to watch for prey. They sing beautiful melodies, usually around dusk. They build their nests with leaves, grass, and mud. They are found mainly in forests or in wooded areas throughout the United States.

1

To draw the wood thrush, begin with a slanted teardrop shape. This will be the bird's body.

2

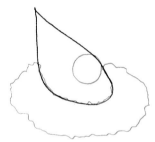

Add a circle near the bottom of the teardrop for the bird's head. Add the wiggly, round shape beneath the bird. This is the outline of the nest.

3

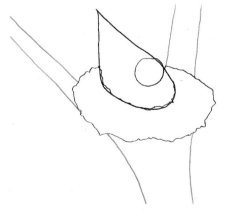

Add the *Y*-shaped tree branch using curved, diagonal lines.

4

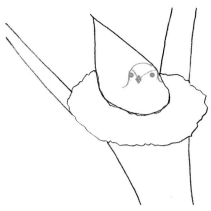

Soften the circle of the bird's head into an upside-down *U*. Add the eyes and the beak. Add details, and erase extra lines.

5

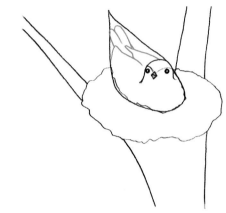

Using curved lines, draw the two wings folded against the bird's back. Add the long tail feathers coming off the bird's backside.

6

Erase extra lines, and add shading and detail. Use heavy, crisscrossing lines for the nest. Don't forget the dark spots on the bird's chest. Add repeating swirly lines to create the look of bark on the tree.

The White House

The White House, located at 1600 Pennsylvania Avenue, is home to the president of the United States. It is 168 feet (51 m) long and 85 ½ feet (26 m) wide. It has 132 rooms, including 16 guest rooms and 35 bathrooms. Architect James Hoban designed the White House. Construction on the building began in 1792. Every U.S. president that came after George Washington has lived in the White House. The White House was one of the buildings burned by the British during the War of 1812. It had to be rebuilt.

Today the building is filled with artwork and furniture that was bought by presidents. The public can visit only a few rooms in the White House. More than one million people visit the White House each year.

1

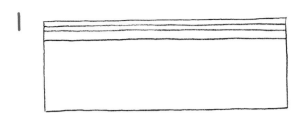

Draw a wide rectangle. Add three horizontal lines across the top.

2

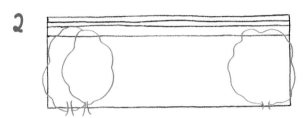

Add three trees to the front of the building. The top of the tree is a cloud shape. The trunks are made with two small, curved lines.

3

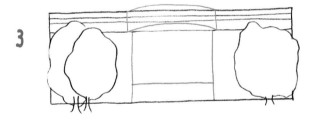

Make the center section of the White House using rectangles and curved lines. Erase the extra lines inside the trees.

4

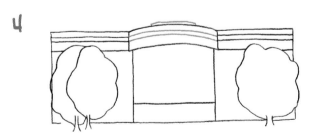

Next add two curved lines across the top section. These should connect the lines on the side of the building. Erase extra horizontal lines inside this section. Add a thin section on the top of the building.

5

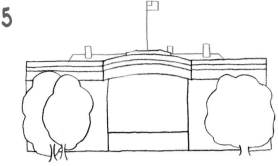

Draw the roof and the chimneys. Draw the American flag in the center of the roof.

6

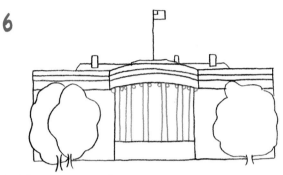

Add columns to the center section using vertical lines and circles.

7

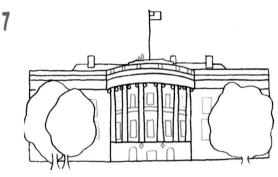

Add the windows, the doors, the railings near the roof, and the other details of the building. Make two security guards on the roof. They protect the president and the staff.

8

Shade your drawing. Wonderful work!

23

Japanese Stone Lanterns

In 1954, Japanese ambassador Sadao Iquichi presented a stone lantern to the United States to mark the one-hundredth anniversary of the first treaty between the United States and Japan. Commodore Matthew C. Perry signed this treaty in 1854. This lantern is now lit each year in the early spring during the opening ceremonies of the National Cherry Blossom Festival. It acts as a reminder of the friendship between Japan and the U.S. Japanese stone lanterns were originally made of metal. They were used to light entrances to shrines and temples. Later the lanterns were made of stone and were used as decorations in gardens. They are carved in many beautiful shapes and styles.

1

Begin by drawing a curved rectangle.

2

Now draw the base of the lantern using curved lines and straight vertical lines.

3

Draw a half circle.

4

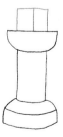

Add two rectangles on top of the half circle. Notice how they give the lantern a three-dimensional look.

5

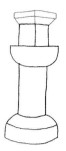

Make four shapes at the top of the lantern.

6

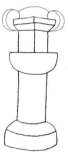

Add the fancy, curved shapes to the top.

7

Carefully draw the shapes at the very top of the lantern. Draw lines where the lantern's details will be.

8

Add shading and detail, and you are done.

25

The Frederick Douglass National Historic Site

Frederick Douglass was an African American born into slavery in 1818. He was one of the most famous African Americans to live during the nineteenth century. After Douglass escaped from slavery, he helped to free other slaves through his writing and his work. When the Civil War (1861–1865) ended, Douglass moved to Washington, D.C. He lived in a house called Cedar Hill from 1877 to 1895. There he continued to work for the equality of African Americans. Today this home is the Frederick Douglass National Historic Site. Most of the furniture is from Douglass's time. Visitors can watch a film about Douglass's life. They can also look at books, view exhibits, and tour Frederick Douglass's home.

Begin with large, rectangular shapes. Notice that each line is slanted at a small angle. This will give the house a three-dimensional shape.

Next add the vertical and slanted lines that will form the borders and edges of the porch.

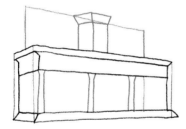

Add the second floor and the bay on top of the porch roof. A bay is an area that has windows and three or more sides. Add columns to the porch using vertical lines.

Add a triangular area above the bay. Draw more diagonal lines to help create the roof. Draw a tiny, round window at the top of the house.

 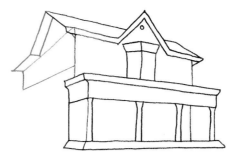

Now begin to work on the side of the house. Notice how it slopes. Erase extra lines.

Draw the lower level of the side of the house. This area has two sections made up of vertical rectangles with small, flat roofs.

Make the windows using rectangles. Add a line at the top of each column. This top section of the column is called a capital.

To finish your drawing, add shading and detail. Notice how the porch area is shadowed.

27

The Capitol

The Capitol in Washington, D.C., is where members of the U.S. government meet to make laws. The building is located on Capitol Hill, near the center of Washington, D.C. Twelve architects contributed to the design of the building. The architect William Thornton was responsible for the original design. Construction of the building began in 1793, and it was completed in 1826. Congress met in the Capitol for the first time on November 17, 1800. The original part of the building is made of sandstone. Over the years, many more additions were made to the building. The dome on top of the building is made of cast iron. It weighs 8,909,200 pounds (4,041,145 kg)! On top of the dome is a bronze statue of the figure of Freedom.

1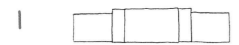

Begin drawing the Capitol by drawing five rectangles. Notice the different heights and sizes of the rectangles.

2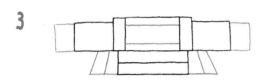

Add two more rectangles in the center of the building.

3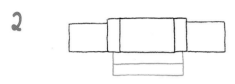

Next draw two horizontal lines in the central rectangle. Add two rectangles to the side. Then add the basic shape of the staircase by making four slanted rectangles.

4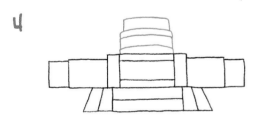

Begin drawing the dome by drawing curved shapes for the dome's base.

5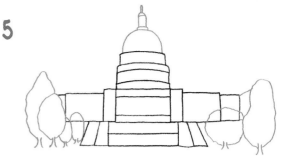

Add a half circle for the dome, and draw a small shape on top of it. Draw a diagonal line for a wing of the building. Add trees.

6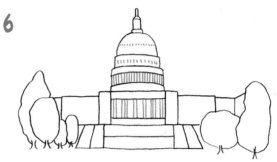

Erase the extra lines. Add detail to the building. Draw small vertical lines for the windows and the columns.

7

Next add more square shapes for the windows. Draw horizontal lines to make the stairs.

8

Add shading to the Capitol to finish your drawing.

District of Columbia Facts

Municipal Corporation	February 21, 1871
Area	68 square miles (176 sq km)
Population	606,900
Industries	Government, tourism
Flower	American Beauty rose
Tree	Scarlet oak
Bird	Wood thrush
Motto	*Justitia Omnibus*, "Justice to All"
Song	"The Star-Spangled Banner"

Glossary

ambassador (am-BA-suh-der) An official that represents his or her country to certain organizations, such as the United Nations.

architect (AR-kih-tekt) Someone who designs buildings.

Civil War (SIH-vul-WOR) The war fought between the northern and southern states of America from 1861 to 1865.

commission (kuh-MIH-shun) A group of people directed to perform a duty.

cupola (KYOO-puh-luh) A small structure built on a roof.

district (DIS-trikt) Part of a certain area, as for governmental purposes.

engineer (en-jih-NEER) A person who is an expert at planning and building bridges and other things.

malaria (muh-LAR-ee-uh) A serious disease common in very warm places, such as Africa.

obelisk (AH-beh-lisk) A tall pillar that ends in a pyramid shape.

prey (PRAY) An animal that is hunted by other animals for food.

quadrants (KWA-druhnts) Four sections.

shrines (SHRYNZ) A special place at which prayers or memorials can be made.

slavery (SLAY-vuh-ree) The system of one person "owning" another.

symbolize (SIM-buh-lyz) To stand for something important.

temples (TEM-puhlz) Buildings dedicated to religious ceremonies or worship.

veto (VEE-toh) The power of one branch or department of a government to refuse approval of laws proposed by another department.

War of 1812 (WOR UV AY-teen TWELV) A war between the United States and Britain, fought from 1812 to 1815.

washing blue (WAH-sheen BLOO) A very fine blue iron powder that is used to prevent white laundry from yellowing.

Index

B
Banneker, Benjamin, 4

C
capital, 4, 12
Capitol, 6, 10, 28
Civil War, 26
Congress, 4, 12, 28

D
district bird, 20
district flag, 14
district flower, 16
district seal, 12
Douglass, Frederick, 26
Dubois, A. E., 14

F
Frederick Douglass National Historic Site, 26

H
Hillyer, Henry Livingston, 8–9
Hoban, James, 22

I
Iquichi, Sadao, 24

J
Jefferson Memorial, 6

L
L'Enfant, Pierre Charles, 4
Lincoln Memorial, 6

P
Perry, Commodore Matthew C., 24
Potomac River, 10

S
scarlet oak, 18

T
Thornton, William, 28
tourism, 6

W
War of 1812, 5, 22
Washington, George, 14, 22
Washington Monument, 6
White House, 5, 22

Web Sites

To learn more about District of Columbia, check out these Web sites:
www.123washingtondc.com
www.district-of-columbia.com